Facts About the Burrowing Owl

By Lisa Strattin

© 2016 Lisa Strattin

Revised © 2019

FREE BOOK

http://LisaStrattin.com/Subscribe-Here

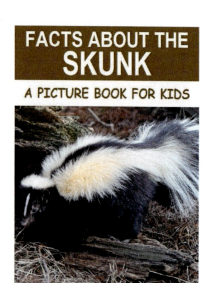

Facts for Kids Picture Books by Lisa Strattin

Pygmy Rabbit, Vol 153

Jumping Rabbit, Vol 154

Mini Rabbits, Vol 155

Blue Quail, Vol 156

Mountain Quail, Vol 157

Quokka, Vol 158

Quoll, Vol 159

Raccoon, Vol 160

Raccoon Dog, Vol 161

Radiated Tortoise, Vol 162

Sign Up for New Release Emails Here

http://LisaStrattin.com/subscribe-here

All rights reserved. No part of this book may be reproduced by any means whatsoever without the written permission from the author, except brief portions quoted for purpose of review.

All information in this book has been carefully researched and checked for factual accuracy. However, the author and publisher makes no warranty, express or implied, that the information contained herein is appropriate for every individual, situation or purpose and assume no responsibility for errors or omissions. The reader assumes the risk and full responsibility for all actions, and the author will not be held responsible for any loss or damage, whether consequential, incidental, special or otherwise, that may result from the information presented in this book.

All images are purchased from stock photo sites or royalty free for commercial use.

I have relied on my own observations as well as many different sources for this book and I have done my best to check facts and give credit where it is due. In the event that any material is used without proper permission, please contact me so that the oversight can be corrected.

Contents

INTRODUCTION 7

CHARACTERISTICS AND HABITS 9

ENEMIES 13

WHEN THEY ARE ACTIVE 15

OWL FACTS 23

INTRODUCTION

The Burrowing Owl, also referred to as the Ground Owl is not like other owls. It does not live in trees; it lives in the ground by taking control of homes abandoned by other animals. While it doesn't usually create the hole, this owl is quite capable of making major improvements to it as needed. It can dig quite effectively using its long legs and powerful feet. It can also be found living inside drainage pipes. The Burrowing Owl is quite opportunistic and will use whatever area it finds for its home.

CHARACTERISTICS AND HABITS

Burrowing Owls are some of the few owls that are active during the day. Their favorite time is dawn or dusk for their hunting. But, because of their size, they like to be done feeding by the time the bigger "owl eating" predators come out late at night.

Since they can see in the daylight, if the evening feed didn't go very well, they have the option of hunting later through the morning hours.

Most Burrowing Owl sightings are during the day. States west of the Mississippi Valley have these owls at least for part of the year. If you have prairie dogs, gophers, voles, grasshoppers, or mice, chances are pretty good that you have this owl around as well.

His favorite habitat is grass lands but he will be adaptable to other areas if a food source is available.

ENEMIES

Like other owls, it is a formidable hunter. But, when this owl is daytime hunting, it forages on the ground, running down insects and lizards. Most of its flight hunting is done during the night just like other owls. Because it hunts on the ground during the daylight hours, snakes, coyotes, foxes, cats and even dogs are all known as its enemies.

WHEN THEY ARE ACTIVE

Burrowing Owls are fascinating birds. There are about two hundred different species of owls and they are found throughout many parts of the world. Most owls are nocturnal (active at night.) Burrowing owls form a different classification from the rest of owls, mainly due to their daytime activity.

Contrary to what most people think, an owl cannot turn its head completely around, but they can turn it around more than people can. Owls are far-sighted they cannot see anything but a few inches away, so once they catch prey they eat it by feel rather than sight. Their eyes are fixed in the sockets, in order to look in a different direction they need to turn their entire head. This is what makes it appear that they can turn their heads all the way around.

In Asia, different owl species are associated with different characteristics; for example the white owl is associated with wealth but the screech owl with evil demons. In Aztec cultures, owls were taboo because they were associated with evil.

They are also commonly seen as wise, this was gleaned from Greek mythology, where the little owl was a friend with Athena, Goddess of birds.

OWL FACTS

Owls are raptors, birds of prey, in the same family as hawks and eagles. They are carnivores, meat-eaters, and they swallow their prey whole. Can you imagine not chewing your food? Owls eat mammals, especially rodents, reptiles, insects and other birds.

Owls live everywhere in the world except Antarctica. The smallest owl is the Elf Owl, which is 4.5 inches tall. The largest owl is the Eurasian Eagle Owl, which grows to be 28 inches tall. Owls have special wings that allow them to fly without making a sound.

COLOR ME

COLOR ME

COLOR ME

COLOR ME

COLOR ME

COLOR ME

COLOR ME

Please leave me a review here:

http://lisastrattin.com/Review-Vol-18

For more Kindle Downloads Visit Lisa Strattin Author Page on Amazon Author Central

http://amazon.com/author/lisastrattin

To see upcoming titles, visit my website at LisaStrattin.com– all books available on kindle!

http://lisastrattin.com

FREE BOOK

http://LisaStrattin.com/Subscribe-Here

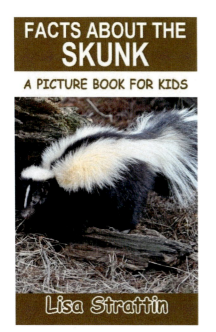

Made in the USA
Columbia, SC
09 March 2021